Wild Weather

Contents

written by Jack Gabolinscy

A tornado is wild weather.
A strong wind starts in the storm clouds.
It blows around and around in a circle.
It lifts up everything that gets in its way.

A tornado can lift up a tree or a car. It can lift the roof right off a house. Sometimes tornadoes are called twisters. A tornado at sea is called a waterspout.

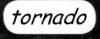

tornado

A hurricane is wild weather from the sea. A big wind blows around in a circle. There is no wind in the middle of the storm. The middle is called the eye of the hurricane.

The hurricane hits the land with heavy rain. Big waves and rain make bad floods. The wind blows down houses and trees. It makes big waves that can sink boats.

hurricane

A cyclone is wild weather.
It starts out in the sea, too.
It is like a very big hurricane.

cyclone

Its winds go in a big circle like a wheel. A cyclone can do a lot of damage when it hits the land.

A thunderstorm is wild weather.
After you see lightning in the sky,
you will hear loud thunder.
It can be scary, but it can't hurt you.

lightning

But a lightning flash is so hot that it can start a forest fire.
Lightning can burn a building down.
It is hotter than the sun!

A hailstorm is wild weather.
When the clouds go very high,
the rain gets frozen into hailstones.

hailstones

The hailstones can hurt people.
They can break the windows of a car.
The biggest ones are as big as a ball.

A snowstorm is wild weather.
A strong wind blows snow everywhere.
Sometimes it is called a blizzard.

snowstorm

In a bad snowstorm you can't see anything but snow.
That is called a whiteout.

A sandstorm is wild weather.
Strong winds in the desert pick up
sand and blow it all around.

sandstorm

People in houses and buildings close the windows and stay inside.
They have to wait until the storm is over.

Wild weather is dangerous.
Storms are stronger than people.
The best place to be is safe at home.